LET YOUR

LIGHT

SHINE

A Devotional & Workbook
Encouraging Kids to Shine Bright

Mandy Fender

Let Your Light Shine ©
Copyright Mandy Fender 2020

THIS BOOK BELONGS TO:

_____

CONTENTS:

JESUS SAID...

"You are the light of the world. A town built on a hill cannot be hidden. Neither do people light a lamp and put it under a bowl. Instead they put it on its stand, and it gives light to everyone in the house. In the same way, let your light shine before others, that they may see your good deeds and glorify your Father in heaven."

Matthew 5:14-16 (NIV)

CAN YOU DRAW A PICTURE
OF A CANDLE SHINING BRIGHT?

BIBLE VERSES ABOUT LIGHT

Genesis 1:3 (NIV) And God said, "Let there be light," and there was light.

Psalm 18:28 (NIV) You, Lord, keep my lamp burning; my God turns my darkness into light.

Psalm 27:1 (NIV) The Lord is my light and my salvation—whom shall I fear? The Lord is the stronghold of my life—of whom shall I be afraid?

Psalm 119:105 (KJV) Thy word is a lamp unto my feet, and a light unto my path.

Matthew 5:16 (NIV) In the same way, let your light shine before others, that they may see your good deeds and glorify your Father in heaven.

Luke 11:36 (NLT) If you are filled with light, with no dark corners, then your whole life will be radiant, as though a floodlight were filling you with light.

John 1:5 (NIV) The light shines in the darkness, and the darkness has not overcome it.

John 8:12 (NIV) When Jesus spoke again to the people, he said, "I am the light of the world. Whoever follows me will never walk in darkness, but will have the light of life."

John 9:5 (NKJV) "As long as I am in the world, I am the light of the world."

John 12:36 (NIV) Believe in the light while you have the light, so that you may become children of light.

Ephesians 5:8 (NIV) For you were once darkness, but now you are light in the Lord. Live as children of light.

1 Peter 2:9 (NIV) But you are a chosen people, a royal priesthood, a holy nation, God's special possession, that you may declare the praises of him who called you out of darkness into his wonderful light.

1 John 1:5 (NIV) This is the message we have heard from him and declare to you: God is light; in him there is no darkness at all.

2 Corinthians 4:6 (NIV) For God, who said, "Let light shine out of darkness," made his light shine in our hearts to give us the light of the knowledge of God's glory displayed in the face of Christ.

Acts 13:47 (NIV) For this is what the Lord has commanded us: "I have made you a light for the Gentiles, that you may bring salvation to the ends of the earth."

Romans 13:12 (NIV) The night is nearly over; the day is almost here. So let us put aside the deeds of darkness and put on the armor of light.

1 Thessalonians 5:5 (NIV) You are all children of the light and children of the day. We do not belong to the night or to the darkness.

DEVOTIONALS

LET THERE BE LIGHT!

Genesis 1:3 (NIV) And God said, "Let there be light," and there was light.

Did you know that God created ALL light? He created the sun, moon, and the stars, and separated the light from the darkness. Have you ever tried to walk in a dark room? It's hard to see anything and you may even run into things, but when you turn on the lights, you can see! God said, "*Let there be...*" and there was! Remember, God can create light! He wants us to walk in the light He created and He will help us when things seem dark, because He will be our light!

Before we can be the light, we must walk in God's light!

PRAYER:

Lord, I pray that I walk in Your light every single day and that You would help me shine bright in Jesus' name! Amen!

NOTES

GOD'S WORD = LIGHT

Psalm 119:105 (KJV) Thy word is a lamp unto my feet, and a light unto my path.

Did you know God's Word, the Bible, is like a lamp? The more you read and ask God to help you understand His Word, the more light you have for the path ahead. Read the Bible every day and hide it in your heart so you always have a lamp ready when you need it, like a flashlight you can use in the darkness. You can shine bright when you have God's Word in your heart and mind!

God's Word helps us to shine bright for Him!

PRAYER:

Lord, help me understand Your Word when I read it in the Bible, and give me a good memory so I can keep it in my heart to shine bright for You. I pray Your Word is my light! In Jesus' name, amen!

:NOTES:

FILLED WITH LIGHT

Luke 11:36 (NIV) Therefore, if your whole body is full of light, and no part of it dark, it will be just as full of light as when a lamp shines its light on you.

God has given us His Light and His Word so that we do not have any darkness hiding in our hearts because He is in our hearts, filling us with His awesome and loving light. When God shines bright within our hearts and helps us in our lives, we can shine bright for Him, and others will see the hope Jesus gives within us.

Allow God to help you make the right choices in your life and, remember, He is the light within your soul!

PRAYER:

Lord, You are the bright light in my heart. Help me keep all darkness out and give me strength to follow You. In Jesus' name, amen!

:NOTES:

JESUS IS THE LIGHT OF THE WORLD

John 8:12 (NIV) When Jesus spoke again to the people, he said, "I am the light of the world. Whoever follows me will never walk in darkness, but will have the light of life."

Jesus said He is the light of the world and whoever follows Him will have the light of life! What do you think that means? It means we will always have hope in Jesus! When we follow Jesus, we will never be in darkness because Jesus is the light. As we walk in this world, we have Jesus leading us and helping us. As long as we follow Him, we will have light and hope!

PRAYER:

Lord, thank You for being the light of the world and for being my hope. Be the light in me. In Jesus' name, amen!

.:NOTES:.

LET YOUR LIGHT SHINE

Matthew 5:16 (NIV) In the same way, let your light shine before others, that they may see your good deeds and glorify your Father in heaven.

Did you know that Jesus wants us to shine bright so others can see His love? When we follow Jesus and love like Him, others will see our good deeds and glorify Him! When we obey our parents, help others, and are kind, we can shine bright and point others to the awesome love of Jesus Christ!

The Bible says do everything as unto the Lord, which means whatever we do, we do for Jesus, and give Him our best. We can love like Him and shine bright because He first loved us. When you do good, point to Jesus and give Him praise!

PRAYER:

Lord, I pray I shine my light bright for You and that You can use me every day to show others Your love. In Jesus' name, amen!

.:NOTES:.

NO LONGER IN DARKNESS

Ephesians 5:8 (NIV) For you were once darkness, but now you are light in the Lord. Live as children of light.

In this verse, we see that, once upon a time, we were all in darkness, because without Jesus, there is no light, but with Jesus, we can now be children of light! This means that we are made new when we believe in Jesus. The Bible even tells us that we are new creatures in Christ and the old things that we did are passed away, because all things have been made new in Jesus.

Put Jesus first in your life and follow Him every day, and walk in the light!

PRAYER:

Lord, thank You for bringing me out of darkness. I pray I put You first and follow You every day. In Jesus' name, amen!

::NOTES::

WONDERFUL
LIGHT

1 Peter 2:9 (NIV) But you are a chosen people, a royal priesthood, a holy nation, God's special possession, that you may declare the praises of him who called you out of darkness into his wonderful light.

God has chosen you! All who call upon the name of the Lord shall be saved and He has called us out of darkness and into His wonderful light. How awesome is that? God loves us so much that He sent Jesus to die for us and, 3 days later, Jesus rose again, so now we have hope in Him! Now, we are no longer in darkness, but in His wonderful light!

Keep trusting God and remember you are special to Him, and He has given you His wonderful light!

PRAYER:

Lord, thank You for calling me out of darkness and into Your wonderful light. Help me overcome and shine bright. In Jesus' name, amen!

.:NOTES:.

LIGHT BEATS DARKNESS

John 1:5 (NIV) The light shines in the darkness, and the darkness has not overcome it.

Did you know that light casts no shadow? There is no darkness in light and light always wins. If you shine a flashlight in a dark room, there is nowhere for the darkness to hide because where ever you shine the light, darkness disappears!

Stay in the light and follow Jesus' example. He will never lead you the wrong way because He knows which way to go and will be your light!

Follow Jesus and know His light always beats the darkness!

PRAYER:

Lord, You are my light and my salvation. Thank You for overcoming the darkness, help me overcome, too! In Jesus' name, amen!

.:NOTES:.

32

JESUS IS THE LIGHT FOR EVERYONE

Acts 13:47 (NIV) "I have made you a light for the Gentiles, that you may bring salvation to the ends of the earth."

Jesus came to save that which was lost. He came to bring salvation to you, and me, and everyone you see! Jesus shares a story about sheep that says He will even leave the 99 to find the 1 who is lost. God is faithful and He wants to bring everyone back to Him because He loves us. He has given us the awesome choice to believe in Him! In the book of Isaiah, it also told us that Jesus would come and be the light, now it's up to us to follow Jesus. Remember, Jesus loves you and He is the light we all need.

PRAYER:

Lord, let me care for others like You care. Thank You for being the light to everyone! In Jesus' name, amen!

.:NOTES:.

NO DARKNESS AT ALL

1 John 1:5 (NIV) This is the message we have heard from him and declare to you: God is light; in him there is no darkness at all.

In the world, there is a lot of darkness, but in God, there is no darkness at all. God will help you shine bright and live uprightly, avoiding the traps of darkness. The Bible says He will make crooked paths straight and that He will help keep our feet from slipping.

Keep your eyes on Jesus and stay focused on His light, not the world's darkness. Because we already know the light of Jesus wins every time!

PRAYER:

Lord, make my crooked paths straight. Help me focus on Your light so I can shine bright. In Jesus' name, amen!

:.NOTES:.

36

CHILDREN OF THE LIGHT

1 Thessalonians 5:5 (NIV) You are all children of the light and children of the day. We do not belong to the night or to the darkness.

We may be in this world, but did you know that we do not belong to this world? We belong to God. God is our Heavenly Father, who is our constant source of strength. He helps us by giving us wisdom to make the right choices, even if they're hard. He gives us peace and hope so we can live in this world without being a part of its darkness.

Remember, the light has overcome darkness. Walk in the light and shine bright for Jesus, offering others the same hope and light you have!

PRAYER:

Lord, help me to remember I am not of this world and that I belong to You. I pray I shine bright for You. In Jesus' name, amen!

:.NOTES:.

SHINE IN OUR HEARTS

2 Corinthians 4:6 (NIV) For God, who said, "Let light shine out of darkness," made his light shine in our hearts to give us the light of the knowledge of God's glory displayed in the face of Christ.

How cool is that?!? God made His light shine in the hearts of people so they could have knowledge of God's glory in the face of Jesus Christ!

I believe God can still shine in our hearts today and though we may not be able to see Jesus face-to-face, the Bible says: blessed are those who have not seen, yet, still believe. Guess what? That's you and me! We have not seen Jesus face-to-face as they did, but we still believe and shine bright for Him! And, one day, we will see Him!

PRAYER:

Lord, shine Your light in my heart and help me be strong in You. In Jesus' name, amen!

.:NOTES:.

THE ARMOR OF LIGHT

Romans 13:12 (NIV) The night is nearly over; the day is almost here. So let us put aside the deeds of darkness and put on the armor of light.

Can you think of another time the Bible mentions armor in the New Testament? Ephesians, that's right! Ephesians 6 says: Stand firm then, with the belt of truth buckled around your waist, with the breastplate of righteousness in place, and with your feet fitted with the readiness that comes from the gospel of peace. In addition to all this, take up the shield of faith, with which you can extinguish all the flaming arrows of the evil one. Take the helmet of salvation and the sword of the Spirit, which is the word of God. Put on the full armor of God to help you overcome darkness and shine bright!

PRAYER:

Lord, help me to keep the full armor You have given me on so that I can overcome and shine bright! In Jesus' name, amen!

.:NOTES:.

BELIEVE IN THE LIGHT JESUS GIVES

John 12:36 (NIV) "Believe in the light while you have the light, so that you may become children of light."

Do you know what Jesus wants us to believe? He wants us to believe in Him and His Word. Everything Jesus said is true and will come to pass. In this verse, Jesus is talking to His disciples and telling them they must believe in the light. Later on, in the same chapter, He says, "I have come into the world as a light, so that no one who believes in me should stay in darkness." Don't live in darkness when Jesus came to bring you light. Jesus doesn't want us to fear, but wants us to trust in Him and shine bright! Believe Jesus is Lord!

PRAYER:

Jesus, I believe in You! Help me to trust You and shine bright. In Jesus' name, amen!

.:NOTES:.

44

SHINE BRIGHT

Matthew 5:14-16 (NIV) "You are the light of the world. A town built on a hill cannot be hidden. Neither do people light a lamp and put it under a bowl. Instead they put it on its stand, and it gives light to everyone in the house. In the same way, let your light shine before others, that they may see your good deeds and glorify your Father in heaven."

For this last devotional, let's remember, we are the light of the world because we have the light of Jesus! Everything we do and say can help others see Jesus in a greater way. The way we speak, help, and treat others can bring glory to God! Never forget to follow Jesus' example. Jesus must increase and we must decrease, meaning we must put God's will above our own. Sometimes, this will be hard, but it will always be worth it, because God's plan is good! Shine bright and let others see Jesus' light!

PRAYER:

Lord, shine bright through me and may what I do in my life bring You glory! In Jesus' name, amen!

.:NOTES:.

ACTIVITIES, FUN FACTS, AND QUESTIONS

IN EACH LIGHT BULB, DRAW OR WRITE DOWN A BRIGHT IDEA!

Did you know God gave the 3 Wise Men a star to follow to get to Jesus? They followed the light so they could get to Jesus and worship Him and give Him gifts of gold, frankincense, and myrrh.

Matthew 2:9-10 (NIV)
…they went on their way, and the star they had seen when it rose went ahead of them until it stopped over the place where the child was. When they saw the star, they were overjoyed.

(You can read the story in Matthew 2.)

Did you know the world cannot live without sunlight?

God placed the earth exactly where it needed to be so we could have enough light!

Did you know the moon shines because it reflects the light of the sun?

May we also shine like the moon, reflecting the light of Jesus Christ, the Son!

CAN YOU GET THE FLOWER TO THE SUN?

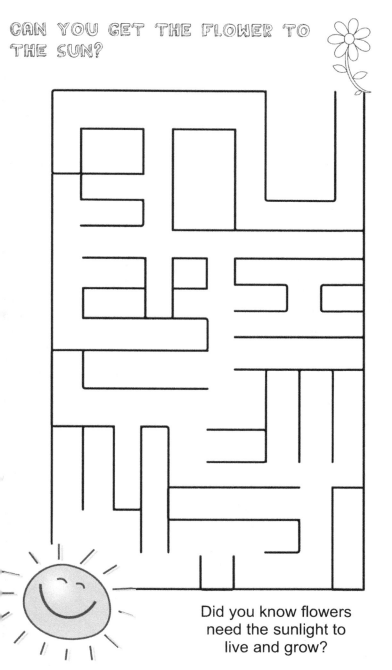

Did you know flowers need the sunlight to live and grow?

WRITE DOWN YOUR FAVORITE BIBLE VERSES ABOUT LIGHT

FILL IN EACH BUBBLE WITH WAYS YOU CAN SHINE BRIGHT:

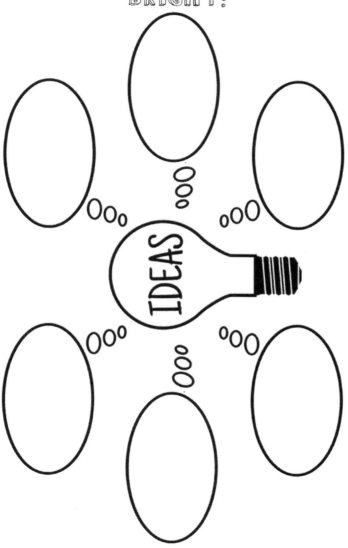

WHAT IS YOUR FAVORITE BIBLE VERSE?

WHAT DAY DID GOD CREATE LIGHT?
(Read Genesis 1 for the answer if you don't already know it.)

WHAT DID GOD CREATE ON DAY 4 OF CREATION?

(Clue: Think about the sky and what is in it.)

DID YOU KNOW LIGHT TRAVELS IN A
COMPLETELY STRAIGHT LINE UNTIL AN
OBJECT MAKES IT BEND?

DID YOU KNOW LIGHT TRAVELS VERY,
VERY FAST?

GUESS HOW FAST...

ANSWER: 186,282
MILES PER SECOND

GENESIS 9:12

I HAVE PLACED MY RAINBOW IN THE CLOUDS. IT IS THE SIGN OF MY COVENANT WITH YOU AND WITH ALL THE EARTH.

DID YOU KNOW A RAINBOW IS A SIGN OF GOD'S PROMISE? WHO DID GOD SHOW A RAINBOW TO FIRST?

(The answer is found in Genesis 9)

JESUS IS YOUR LIGHT FOREVER!

THE SUN WILL NO LONGER BE YOUR LIGHT BY DAY, NOR WILL THE BRIGHTNESS OF THE MOON SHINE ON YOU, FOR THE LORD WILL BE YOUR EVERLASTING LIGHT.

Isaiah 60:19

SHINE BRIGHT!

GENESIS 1:4 (NIV)

GOD SAW THAT THE LIGHT WAS GOOD, AND HE SEPARATED THE LIGHT FROM THE DARKNESS.

LET YOUR LIGHT SHINE!

FOR THE NEXT WEEK, KEEP TRACK OF HOW YOU SHINE BRIGHT. USE THE FOLLOWING PAGES TO WRITE DOWN HOW YOU SHINED BRIGHT IN YOUR DAY!

HOW DID YOU SHINE BRIGHT TODAY?

DATE:_____

:.NOTES:.

HOW DID YOU SHINE BRIGHT TODAY?

DATE:_____

.:NOTES:.

HOW DID YOU SHINE BRIGHT TODAY?

DATE:_____

:.NOTES:.

HOW DID YOU SHINE BRIGHT TODAY?

DATE:_____

:NOTES:.

HOW DID YOU SHINE BRIGHT TODAY?

DATE:_____

:.NOTES:.

HOW DID YOU SHINE BRIGHT TODAY?

DATE:_____

:.NOTES:.

90

HOW DID YOU SHINE BRIGHT TODAY?

DATE:_____

:.NOTES:.

SHINE BRIGHT PRAYER

LORD, HELP ME SHINE BRIGHT IN ALL THAT I DO SO OTHERS MAY SEE YOUR LOVE AND LIGHT AND SEEK YOU, TOO!

IN JESUS' NAME, AMEN!

.:NOTES:.

REMEMBER, GOD IS LOVE
AND HE LOVES YOU!

Never stop shining!
Always shine bright!

DEAR READER,

THANK YOU SO MUCH FOR READING! I PRAY THAT YOU ALWAYS KNOW JESUS LOVES YOU. REMEMBER, JESUS IS THE WAY, TRUTH, AND LIFE! HE WILL BE YOUR LIGHT FOREVER. MAY YOU ALWAYS SHINE BRIGHT FOR HIM!

SINCERELY,
MANDY FENDER

STAY BRIGHT!

LET YOUR LIGHT SHINE!

Made in the USA
Las Vegas, NV
17 August 2021